S0-CFU-767

This journal belongs to

_____

AN AQUARIAN EXPOSITION:

3 DAYS OF PEACE & MUSIC

August 15, 16, and 17, 1969. Woodstock Music & Art Fair organizers expected 50,000 attendees. They'd had trouble securing a venue until dairy farmer Max Yasgur agreed to let them use his 600-acre farm in Bethel, New York. Until April, they'd also had trouble signing popular performers. But when the festival began, more than 400,000 attendees arrived. By the time it ended, 32 of the most iconic rock and folk acts of the 1960s had taken the stage. They played in the sun, the rain, and the middle of the night. Rock & roll legends were created, a generation was defined, and music was changed forever.

FRIDAY

5:07	Richie Havens
7:10	invocation from Swami Satchidananda
7:30	Sweetwater
8:20	Bert Sommer
9:20	Tim Hardin
10:00	Ravi Shankar
10:50	Melanie
11:55	Arlo Guthrie
12:55	Joan Baez

SATURDAY

12:15	Quill
1:00	Country Joe McDonald
2:00	Santana
3:30	John Sebastian
4:45	Keef Hartley Band
6:00	The Incredible String Band
7:30	Canned Heat
9:00	Mountain
10:30	Grateful Dead
12:30	Creedence Clearwater Revival
2:00	Janis Joplin with the Kozmic Blues Band
3:30	Sly and the Family Stone
5:00	The Who
8:00	Jefferson Airplane

SUNDAY

2:00	Joe Cocker and the Grease Band
6:30	Country Joe and the Fish
8:15	Ten Years After
10:00	The Band
12:00	Johnny Winter
1:30	Blood, Sweat & Tears
3:00	Crosby, Stills, Nash & Young
6:00	Paul Butterfield Blues Band
7:30	Sha Na Na
9:00	Jimi Hendrix/Gypsy Sun & Rainbows

"I SAY, FOLLOW YOUR BLISS AND DON'T BE AFRAID, AND DOORS WILL OPEN WHERE YOU DIDN'T KNOW THEY WERE GOING TO BE."

—JOSEPH CAMPBELL

LOVERS * DREAMERS * ARTISTS * ANGELS * LOVERS *

LOVERS * DREAMERS * ARTISTS * ANGELS * LOVERS *

PEACE * LOVE * MUSIC

PEACE * LOVE * MUSIC

PEACE * LOVE * MUSIC

"I'M NOT WORRIED ABOUT THE SECURITY PARTICULARLY.
IF PEOPLE HAVE ENOUGH TO DO, THERE WON'T BE TROUBLE."

—WESLEY A. POMEROY, HEAD OF SECURITY AT WOODSTOCK

PEACE * LOVE * MUSIC

PEACE * LOVE * MUSIC

"[IN THE 1960s] WE WERE YOUNG, WE WERE RECKLESS, ARROGANT, SILLY, HEAD-
STRONG ... AND WE WERE RIGHT! I REGRET NOTHING!"

—ABBIE HOFFMAN

LOVERS * DREAMERS * ARTISTS * ANGELS * LOVERS *

LOVERS * DREAMERS * ARTISTS * ANGELS * LOVERS *

DREAMERS * ARTISTS * ANGELS * LOVERS * DREAMERS

DREAMERS * ARTISTS * ANGELS * LOVERS * DREAMERS

PEACE * LOVE * MUSIC * PEACE * LOVE * MUSIC

PEACE * LOVE * MUSIC * PEACE * LOVE * MUSIC

"THINK FOR YOURSELF AND QUESTION AUTHORITY."

—TIMOTHY LEARY

REAMERS * ARTISTS * ANGELS * LOVERS * DREAMERS

REAMERS * ARTISTS * ANGELS * LOVERS * DREAMERS

PEACE * LOVE * MUSIC * PEACE * LOVE * MUSIC

PEACE * LOVE * MUSIC * PEACE * LOVE * MUSIC

"PEACE CAN BE MADE ONLY BY THOSE WHO ARE PEACEFUL,
AND LOVE CAN BE SHOWN ONLY BY THOSE WHO LOVE."

—Alan Watts

PEACE * LOVE * MUSIC

PEACE * LOVE * MUSIC

PEACE * LOVE * MUSIC

"LIKE WOW, THESE PEOPLE ARE REALLY BEAUTIFUL,
THE COPS, THE STOREKEEPERS, THE ARMY, EVERYBODY."

—LAURA GLAZER, A WOODSTOCK ATTENDEE

LOVERS * DREAMERS * ARTISTS * ANGELS * LOVERS *

LOVERS * DREAMERS * ARTISTS * ANGELS * LOVERS *

DREAMERS * ARTISTS * ANGELS * LOVERS * DREAMERS

DREAMERS * ARTISTS * ANGELS * LOVERS * DREAMERS

PEACE * LOVE * MUSIC * PEACE * LOVE * MUSIC

"DON'T BOTHER MAX'S COWS. LET THEM MOO IN PEACE."

—SIGN AT WOODSTOCK

LOVERS * DREAMERS * ARTISTS * ANGELS * LOVERS *

LOVERS * DREAMERS * ARTISTS * ANGELS * LOVERS *

PEACE * LOVE * MUSIC * PEACE * LOVE * MUSIC * PEACE * LOVE * MUSIC

"GOOD MORNING! WHAT WE HAVE IN MIND IS BREAKFAST IN BED FOR 400,000."

—WAVY GRAVY, SPEAKING FROM THE STAGE

PEACE * LOVE * MUSIC * PEACE * LOVE * MUSIC * PEACE * LOVE * MUSIC

"THE WHOLE THING IS A GAS. I DIG IT ALL,
THE MUD, THE RAIN, THE MUSIC, THE HASSLES."

—Speed, A Woodstock attendee

PEACE * LOVE * MUSIC * PEACE * LOVE * MUSIC * PEACE * LOVE * MUSIC

"THE IMPORTANT THING THAT YOU'VE PROVEN TO THE WORLD IS THAT A HALF A MILLION KIDS—AND I CALL YOU KIDS BECAUSE I HAVE CHILDREN THAT ARE OLDER THAN YOU—A HALF MILLION YOUNG PEOPLE CAN GET TOGETHER AND HAVE THREE DAYS OF FUN AND MUSIC AND HAVE NOTHING BUT FUN AND MUSIC, AND I GOD BLESS YOU FOR IT!"

—MAX YASGUR

PEACE * LOVE * MUSIC * PEACE * LOVE * MUSIC * PEACE * LOVE * MUSIC

ISBN 978-1-64178-024-7

COPY PERMISSION: The written instructions, photographs, designs, patterns, and projects in this publication are intended for the personal use of the reader and may be reproduced for that purpose only. Any other use, especially commercial use, is forbidden under law without the written permission of the copyright holder.
NOTE: The use of products and trademark names is for informational purposes only, with no intention of infringement upon those trademarks.

Fox Chapel Publishing makes every effort to use environmentally friendly paper for printing.

We are always looking for talented authors and artists. To submit an idea, please send a brief inquiry to acquisitions@foxchapelpublishing.com.

© 2018 Woodstock Ventures, LC. Under License to Epic Rights/Perryscope Productions LLC and Quiet Fox Designs, an imprint of Fox Chapel Publishing, 800-457-9112, 903 Square Street, Mount Joy, PA 17552.

Printed in China
First printing